GET

ORGANIZED !

FISKE'S UNBEATABLE SYSTEM FOR APPLYING TO COLLEGE

Edward B. Fiske and Phyllis Steinbrecher

Peterson's Guides

Princeton, New Jersey

ISBN 0-87866-995-7

Composition and design by Peterson's Guides

Printed in the United States of America

10 9 8 7 6 5 4 3 2 1

CONTENTS

PREFACE

Get Organized! was created to help high school students feel comfortable with the college admissions process. Its step-by-step approach to the process—which entails much more than merely filling out forms—is designed to take the stress out of the task by clearly laying out what you need to do and when. If you begin to use *Get Organized!* as you begin your junior year, it will help you focus your time and energy on winning an offer of admission from a college of your choice.

> Edward B. Fiske
> Phyllis Steinbrecher
> January 1990

INTRODUCTION

With more than 3,000 two- and four-year colleges and universities in the United States, there are dozens of schools where you could be comfortable and happy. Your job in the next few months is to narrow down that list to the seven or so that are the best for you, make all the deadlines, take the right tests, and do the work necessary to stay in the running for admission to them. Sound impossible? It's not.

Get Organized! will help you get the job done. It's designed to make the process of getting into a college of your choice a manageable task. The key to success lies in your ability to organize yourself and to follow a sensible timetable. Your willingness to keep your mind open to the many options that are available to you also plays an important role.

To begin, take a quick look through the whole workbook. At the front, you'll find a calendar that runs from September of your junior year through June of your senior year. By noting the milestones of these important two years, it sets up a schedule for you to work with. On the inside back cover you'll find the Application Checklist. It's a chart that lays out in an easy-to-use grid the steps that must be taken to apply to any college. Used together, the calendar and checklist allow you to monitor your progress and be on top of your schedule—the keys to staying organized!

A Sense of Perspective

There's no question that selecting the group of colleges that is right for you can be difficult, but it also can be an experience that helps you grow. A successful search requires time, thought, organization, action, and a sense of perspective. Through it you can learn a great deal about yourself—your needs, abilities, and goals—which alone can make the process well worth the effort.

Start as early in the application process as possible with a realistic self-assessment and an honest set of objectives, then compile a list of the twenty or more colleges and universities that offer the academic challenge and social climate you seek. Photocopy the calendar and fill in the days to coincide with the current calendar year. Circle important dates as they become known to you and note what they are in the box for that day. Put the calendar where you will see it daily. Check it regularly to keep track of deadlines. Use the Application Checklist as a timeline, filling it out to mark your progress.

If you approach the admissions process intelligently, armed with information about yourself and the colleges you're interested in, you'll considerably increase your chances of getting into the one you really would like to attend. There's no substitute for organization, persistence, and critical thinking.

It's time to get organized!

YOUR COLLEGE CALENDAR

The twenty-two monthly calendars that appear on the next eleven pages will help you stay on top of the process of applying to college. Being organized is the key to that process, and knowing what you should be doing when helps you get that way.

The calendars begin with September of your junior year and end with June of your senior year. Each month is bulleted with the things that need to be done to move you along at a timely, painless pace.

To use this element of *Get Organized!*, photocopy the pages and fill in the days of the week to coincide with the current calendar year. Circle important dates—SAT registration, the dates of other tests, interview appointments, and application deadlines, for instance—with brightly colored ink and note what they are in the box for that date.

Keep the calendar handy and on display in your room, if possible. Refer to it often and use it in conjunction with the Application Checklist located on the inside back cover.

Lastly, don't worry. Getting organized is easy. The first step is to get going, and that you've already done!

JUNIOR YEAR

September

SUN	MON	TUES	WED	THURS	FRI	SAT

- Check your junior and senior courses. Will you meet college requirements?
- Be sure you are involved in one or two extracurricular activities.

October

SUN	MON	TUES	WED	THURS	FRI	SAT

- Be sure you have a Social Security number. If you don't have one, get one.
- Register for the PSAT.
- Take the PSAT.

- Work to get the best grades you can. The payoff of a strong effort now will be a better shot at getting into a college of your choice.

November

SUN	MON	TUES	WED	THURS	FRI	SAT

- Get involved in a community service activity.
- Begin to read newspapers and a weekly news magazine.
- Buy an SAT prep book and begin to work in it for 15 minutes a night.

December

SUN	MON	TUES	WED	THURS	FRI	SAT

January

SUN	MON	TUES	WED	THURS	FRI	SAT

- Review your PSAT scores.
- Decide with your guidance counselor when to take the ACT, SAT, and/or Achievement Tests (and what Achievements to take).
- Keep your grades up!

February

SUN	MON	TUES	WED	THURS	FRI	SAT

- Plan a challenging schedule of classes for your senior year.

- Register for the tests you will take this spring (ACT, SAT, and Achievements).
- Meet with your guidance counselor to discuss college choices.

SUN	MON	TUES	WED	THURS	FRI	SAT

March

- Take any tests you have registered for.
- Develop a preliminary list of fifteen to twenty colleges and universities and send for information from them.
- Create a folder for each college on your list.
- Continue community service and/or extracurricular activities.

April

SUN	MON	TUES	WED	THURS	FRI	SAT

May

SUN	MON	TUES	WED	THURS	FRI	SAT

- Take the tests you have registered for.
- Plan college visits and call now to make June through October appointments.
- Structure your summer plans to include advanced academic work, travel, volunteer work, or a job.

June

SUN	MON	TUES	WED	THURS	FRI	SAT

- Take the tests you have registered for.
- Do well on your finals.
- Make sure your fall schedule is set.
- Begin to consider which teachers might write good recommendations on your behalf, and ask them if they'd be willing to do so.

- Start visiting campuses. (Don't forget to write thank-you letters to your interviewers and to fill out college visit summary sheets.)
- Begin to think about your essay.

July

SUN	MON	TUES	WED	THURS	FRI	SAT

- Continue campus visits.
- Draft your main essay.
- Write to request application forms from the colleges and universities you are interested in.

August

SUN	MON	TUES	WED	THURS	FRI	SAT

SENIOR YEAR

September

SUN	MON	TUES	WED	THURS	FRI	SAT

- Register for the ACT, SAT, and Achievements, as necessary.
- Wrap up campus visits.
- Check with your counselor for the fall visiting schedule of college reps.
- Continue to work on essay drafts.
- Meet with your counselor to compile your final list of schools.
- Ask teachers to get your recommendations ready. Let them know what is due when, and where.
- Keep your grades up.

October

SUN	MON	TUES	WED	THURS	FRI	SAT

- Mail early applications after carefully checking them.
- Take the tests you have registered for.
- Familiarize yourself with the exact processes by which transcripts and applications go out.
- Be aware of all deadlines.
- Photocopy all the application forms before you fill them out. Use the duplicate as a worksheet.
- Have your counselor or English teacher check your essays.
- Review for any tests you'll be taking.

- Be sure you have filled out the forms that are necessary to ensure ACT, SAT, and Achievement scores will be sent to your colleges of choice.
- Check that the people who are writing recommendations make their deadlines.
- Be sure your transcript has been sent to your colleges of choice.
- Complete all applications. Make copies of *everything*. Put duplicates in their corresponding folders.

November

SUN	MON	TUES	WED	THURS	FRI	SAT

- Take any necessary ACT, SAT, and Achievement Tests. This is the only month in which the English Composition with Essay Achievement (required by many colleges) is given.
- Meet with your counselor to verify that all is in order and out to colleges.

December

SUN	MON	TUES	WED	THURS	FRI	SAT

January

SUN	MON	TUES	WED	THURS	FRI	SAT

- Prepare Financial Aid Form (FAF) or Family Financial Statement (FFS).
- Check with everyone who has written a recommendation for you to make sure the letters have gone to the right places.

February

SUN	MON	TUES	WED	THURS	FRI	SAT

- Be sure your midyear report goes to every college to which you've applied.
- Send in your FAF or FFS.
- Write to let your colleges know of any new honors or accomplishments.

- Register for any Advanced Placement tests you may be taking.
- Be sure you have received FAF or FFS acknowledgments.

			March			
SUN	MON	TUES	WED	THURS	FRI	SAT

- Review the acceptances and financial aid offers you receive.
- Go back to visit one or two of your top-choice schools, then make your final decision.
- Notify your college of choice of your acceptance of its offer.
- Be sure your deposit is received by the school you've chosen *before* May 1.
- Notify the schools you have chosen not to attend of your decision.

			April			
SUN	MON	TUES	WED	THURS	FRI	SAT

May

SUN	MON	TUES	WED	THURS	FRI	SAT

- Take AP exams.

June

SUN	MON	TUES	WED	THURS	FRI	SAT

- Graduate proudly! Congratulations on a fine job of completing the college application process.

ON YOUR MARK

Finding the right college requires two steps at the outset. You must know yourself and you must identify the characteristics of a college or university that are most important to you.

This section shows you how to do both and, in the process, helps you begin to get organized. Get your pencil out and ready, and let's get started.

GETTING TO KNOW YOURSELF

It is important to trust yourself and your instincts when choosing a college. Those instincts work best when you have a clear understanding of your needs and goals, and the first step in that direction is self-evaluation. In order to clarify your thinking, write down your thoughts in response to the following questions.

Ten Questions to Get You Thinking

1. What extracurricular activities do you enjoy most? Which have given you the greatest pleasure and sense of accomplishment? Are there activities you have *not* been involved in during your high school years that you might like to pursue in college?

2. Which subjects in school interest you most? Least?

> **See your guidance counselor in your junior year and work closely with him or her throughout this process.**

3. Do you enjoy being thrust into new situations with new people, or do you prefer the familiar? How easily do you adjust to new situations?

4. What five adjectives best describe you as an individual? What sets you apart from other people?

5. How would your best friend describe you? What would he or she say your strengths and weaknesses are?

6. How would one of your teachers describe you as an individual and as a member of the community?

7. What makes you feel happy? Angry? Satisfied? Frustrated? Anxious? Involved?

8. Where do you want to be twenty years from now? What would you like to be doing?

9. What events or experiences in your life have been most important to you so far? Why?

10. How do you react to competitive academic and social situations?

YOUR PERSONAL DATA SHEET

Every college requires you, the applicant, to provide factual information about yourself. Begin to compile your personal data now, and fill in certain information (such as SAT scores) as it becomes available. Using the form that begins below and continues on the next five pages will keep the information in one place and make completing individual applications easier later on. In addition, putting certain things down on paper—information about your school, extracurricular activities, community service, and work experience—gives you a list of your strengths, talents, and interests and can help in the process of self-awareness.

Personal Data

Name _____

Address _____

Phone number _____

Parents:

    Father _____

    Mother's maiden name _____

High School:

    Name _____

    Address _____

Phone number _____

Guidance counselor _____

CEEB number* _____

	Junior Year	*Senior Year*
Grade Point Average	_____	_____
Class Rank	_____	_____

Test Scores

PSAT					
SAT					
ACH					
ACT					

Awards and Honors

_____

_____

_____

_____

_____

*This identification number, given to your high school by the College Board, is available from your guidance counselor.

Extracurricular Activities

Sports

_____

_____

_____

_____

Clubs

_____

_____

_____

_____

Drama

_____

_____

_____

_____

Art

_____

_____

_____

_____

Music   _____

           _____

           _____

           _____

Other   _____

           _____

           _____

           _____

Work Experience

(List where you worked, for how long, and what you did. Give the name and phone number of anyone who could give you a recommendation.)

1.

2.

3.

Community Service

(List where you worked, for how long, and what you did. Give the name and phone number of anyone who could give you a recommendation.)

1.

2.

3.

Travel

(List any travel or related experiences, such as an Outward Bound experience or a bike trip through New England, you feel were relevant to your personal growth.)

1.

2.

3.

4.

Special Situations

Minority status _____

Alumni relationships _____

_____

_____

_____

Geographic preference_____

_____

_____

_____

WHAT YOU'RE LOOKING FOR IN A COLLEGE

The questions below will help you get a feel for what you are looking for in a college or university. Circle your answer, or, where appropriate, put your thoughts down in writing.

1. Do you want a liberal arts college, technical institution, or comprehensive university? (Circle one)

2. What size school feels right for you? Less than 1,000 students, 1,000–5,000, 5,000–10,000, more than 10,000. (Circle one)

3. Would you like to live in a city, suburb, small town, or rural area? (Circle one)

4. Would you like to live far from or close to home? (Circle one)

5. Would you like to live in a familiar area or in a totally different part of the United States? Where?

6. Which of the following interest you? Fraternities and sororities; big-time sports; good intramural sports; intense academics and strong competition; independent study options; overseas study opportunities; strong art, music, or drama programs; a laid-back atmosphere; opportunity for close faculty-student relationships; religious affiliation; or military affiliation. (Circle all that apply)

7. What special programs (engineering, business, science, or creative writing, for instance) interest you? (List)

8. List below any other aspects of college life that are important to you.

Now Sit Down . . .

Take the two exercises you've completed—your personal data sheet and your thoughts on what type of college interests you—as well as information you've gathered from your guidance counselor, up-to-date college guides, teachers, parents, and friends, and put together a preliminary list of twenty or so colleges and universities to consider. Send for catalogs (also called viewbooks) and application forms from the institutions, using postcards or letters.

Your List

1. _____
2. _____
3. _____
4. _____
5. _____
6. _____
7. _____
8. _____
9. _____
10. _____
11. _____
12. _____
13. _____
14. _____
15. _____
16. _____
17. _____
18. _____
19. _____
20. _____

Sample Letter for Requesting a Catalog and Application Form

Your Street Address
Town, State, Zip Code
Date

Director of Admissions
College Name
Address
Town, State, Zip Code

Dear Sir or Madam:

I am a junior at (name of your high school) and will graduate in (month and year of graduation). I hope to begin college in (month and year) and would appreciate any information you could send me about (name of college).

Please also send any other relevant information, including application and financial aid forms. I am especially interested in (indicate a major and/or extracurricular activities), and would appreciate information about them too.

Thank you for your help. I look forward to hearing from you soon.

Sincerely,

(signature)
Your Name

HOW TO ORGANIZE INCOMING MATERIAL

Soon you'll be receiving lots of information from colleges, solicited *and* unsolicited. Some will interest you; some will not. But scan everything to make sure you don't overlook one that you might not have thought about.

Set up a separate, clearly marked folder for each college that interests you. Put any material you receive in its respective folder as soon as you receive it. Don't throw anything away until you are *positive* you won't be applying there. *Mark important dates* for the colleges you are interested in on the Application Checklist (inside back cover) as soon as you know them. Set up a single file with all of the individual folders in alphabetical order.

> **Read college catalogs as soon as you get them to find out which colleges require interviews and the date they must be held by.**

Now that you've begun to gather information about the colleges and universities that interest you, it's time to get serious about what you need to do to meet all the requirements and make all the deadlines to keep in the running as an applicant. On the pages that follow, you'll find a rundown of the commonly required standardized tests, questions to help you prepare for campus visits, and a method for organizing your findings after the interview is over.

A WORD ABOUT STANDARDIZED TESTS

Most colleges require applicants to take a number of standardized tests and submit their scores. Check the information you have received from the schools you are interested in to find out what tests they require. Write them down in the appropriate spaces on the Application Checklist, which you'll find on the back inside cover. Registration forms and lists of test dates and centers are available in the guidance office of your high school. For information on Achievement Tests, the PSAT, or SAT, contact: College Board Admissions Testing Program (ETS), Box 6200, Princeton, New Jersey 08541-6200, 609-771-7600. For information about the ACT, contact: American College Testing Program, 2201 North Dodge Street, P.O. Box 168, Iowa City, Iowa 52243, 319-337-1000.

PSAT: The PSAT (Preliminary Scholastic Aptitude Test) is a 2-hour multiple-choice test given in October as a practice test to familiarize juniors (or sophomores) with the SAT. Results are reported in detail, so strengths and weaknesses can be easily assessed. The

> **Make sure you have the high school courses to meet the requirements of your colleges of choice.**

PSAT also serves as the National Merit Scholarship Qualifying Test (NMSQT), through which students who take the PSAT/NMSQT can be designated National Merit Scholars, Finalists, Semifinalists, or Commended Students.

SAT: The SAT (Scholastic Aptitude Test) is a 3-hour multiple-choice test in two sections: verbal and mathematics. The verbal section is designed to test reading comprehension and vocabulary. The math section tests the ability to solve problems involving arithmetical reasoning, algebra, and geometry. The SAT also includes the Test of Standard Written English (TSWE), which tests knowledge of the mechanics of written English. The SAT is usually offered five times throughout the year and should be taken at least twice, once in the spring of junior year and once in the fall of senior year.

Achievement Tests: Achievement Tests are designed to test knowledge in specific subject areas. Tests are offered in fifteen subject areas and are each an hour long. You may take up to three tests on any given test date and may decide the order to take them in. Many students schedule Achievements to coincide with the completion of course requirements in the subject areas to be tested.

ACT: The American College Testing Program Assessment used to be required primarily by midwestern and southern colleges and universities but is being accepted by more and more northeastern institutions. The ACT tests four areas: English, mathematics, reading, and science reasoning. The tests are designed to assess educational development and readiness to handle college-level work. Each area is scored separately; a composite score is also given. Many colleges now ask for the SAT and three Achievements, *or* the ACT.

Worth Noting

Test registration deadlines are printed in all registration booklets. Register for each test well before the deadline. Use the College Calendar to record test dates and the Test Scorecard (on the last page of this book) to record your results.

Fee waivers for all standardized tests are available from your counselor. Check to see if you meet the financial guidelines.

Scores will automatically be sent to the colleges you are applying to *if you designate their names on the test registration forms.* If you do not fill in those names, *you* will be responsible for getting the scores to them at a later date.

CEEB numbers are given by the College Board to every high school in the United States as identification for SAT and Achievement testing. This number is usually posted in your guidance office (if not, your counselor has it) and is requested on many college application forms. Record your high school's CEEB number on your personal data sheets.

To prep or not to prep? That is the question—and it's a big one. There is serious debate as to whether or not prepping for these tests helps to raise scores, though common sense dictates that establishing familiarity with a test is likely to be helpful. Many schools offer classes for that purpose, and private courses and tutoring are usually available. There are also a number of prep books on the market that can be quite helpful. The decision to prep should be an individual one. If you choose to go for it, remember that to succeed you must be committed to putting time into studying.

VISITING COLLEGE CAMPUSES

From reading and discussions with your guidance counselor, parents, and friends, you by now have developed a list of colleges and universities that you are considering applying to.

Visiting colleges can give you a better idea about their educational programs, faculty, facilities, student body, school spirit, and general atmosphere. If a college is a clear first choice, get to that campus. But you do not need to visit every college to which you are planning to apply. Some colleges require an interview as part of the admissions process, most do not. If the colleges you are interested in are too far away to visit, you can get an idea of what they might be like by visiting the ones in your area that are similar.

Tips for Campus Visits

> **In the late spring of your junior year, schedule campus visits for summer and fall.**

* *Read the materials sent by each college.* The college catalog is a description of the academics and atmosphere at the institution. It includes the size of the student body, male-female ratio, admissions requirements, a history of the school, social organizations, and athletics programs. It is often less-than-fascinating reading, but it can give you some valuable information.

* *Select five or six colleges to visit.* It's best to include a large institution, a smaller one, one in a city, and one with a campus setting. This will help you to confirm or change your ideas about what you want. Know the questions you want to ask at each.

* *Look at college and family calendars.* Choose dates and times that everyone can work with. Never schedule visits to more than

two schools in one day. Allow at least 2 hours for each college, as well as time for travel between them. Have alternate dates ready in case your first choice is unavailable.

- *Call in advance to set up your interview appointment.* Calling for an appointment four to six weeks before the date you want is a good rule of thumb. For September and October visits, however, you should make the appointment about eight weeks in advance.

- *Include a tour of the campus.* If possible, try to do the tour before your interview. It will give you a feel for the college or university before you meet with a member of the admissions staff. You might also want to arrange meetings with coaches, department heads, professors, or friends attending the school.

- *Visit while the institution is in session.* It is difficult to get a sense of atmosphere when students aren't around. But if your fall schedule is hectic, use the summer for your initial visits and interviews, and revisit the campuses after you've been accepted.

Once You're There

Visit the library: take note of its accessibility and size.

Visit the dorms, athletics fields, classrooms, and student center.

Stop and talk with students all over campus.

Do some snooping around to places not included on the regular tour.

Read bulletin boards to get a sense of what is happening on campus.

Have a snack in the cafeteria or the student union and listen to the conversations around you.

SURVIVING THE INTERVIEW

For many students, the most worrisome part of applying to college is the personal interview. It needn't be, especially if you are familiar with the two subjects most likely to be discussed: the college and you. Reread the college catalog, your responses in the "Getting to Know Yourself" section, and your personal data sheet before each interview. Below are some tips to help you come through the experience like a pro.

- Be on time! If you are chronically late, allow for plenty of extra time.

- Be yourself. Don't try to be someone you are not.

- Speak clearly. Don't mumble when asking or answering questions, and maintain eye contact.

- Relax! An interview is an exchange of information, not something you pass or fail. Your presence on the campus and your readiness to talk about yourself and your college plans are indications of your seriousness. The interview can help you determine if that college is the right place for you. The exchange of information and the impressions gained on both sides—yours and the interviewer's—should be meaningful.

- Be prepared. The interviewer may encourage you to "just talk," so you should be ready to discuss topics ranging from the very general ("Tell me about your school experience") to the very specific ("How do you feel about nuclear disarmament or capital punishment?").

- Respond directly and articulately to questions. Keep the "you knows" to a minimum—none, if you can help it. It is perfectly all right to say "I don't know" or "I need to think about that" in response to a question. Be as natural, easy, and responsive as you can.

- Be familiar with your academic record. This will enable you to answer general questions about your academic performance in high school and your scores on standardized tests—if asked.

- Know your interests and your areas of strength. Look over your list of extracurricular activities and be prepared to talk about them. Bring up any qualifications you have that may not be apparent from the application.

- Have plausible explanations for any weaknesses in your record. Remember, an explanation is different from an excuse.

- Be prepared to discuss one or two books you have read. Think about why they meant something to you.

- Be aware of current events.

- Thank the interviewer before you leave.

Questions to Expect

A large part of being prepared is knowing what to expect. The questions below are typical of the kinds of questions college interviewers ask. Write out your answers in the space provided.

1. How would you like to see yourself grow over the next four years?

2. What might your teachers say is your greatest strength as a person? As a student? What are your shortcomings in those areas?

3. Do you have a hero or heroine? Who—and why?

4. If you could reach for a telephone and talk to any living person, whom would you call? Why?

5. Have you ever thought of not going to college? What might you do instead?

6. What sets you apart as an individual?

Check to see if representatives from your choice colleges will be visiting your high school.

7. If your best friend was asked to describe you, what would he or she say?

8. What events this year have made you feel indignant? Involved?

9. What do you do in your spare time?

10. If you could ask one, two, or three people to dinner, whom would you invite and why?

11. Why are you considering this college?

12. What do you enjoy reading? What books did you read this year that influenced your thinking? What newspapers and magazines do you read regularly?

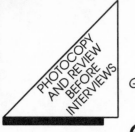

Questions to Ask

At some point in almost every interview, you will be asked if you have any questions. There are no perfect questions; the best ones are those you want the answer to. Below are examples of the kinds of questions students ask.

1. When must I declare a major? Is it difficult to switch?

2. Do senior faculty members teach freshmen?

3. Which departments are considered the strongest on this campus?

4. Are off-campus programs available for credit? Co-op programs? Internships? Study abroad? Intercollege exchange?

5. How diverse is the student body? Does one group dominate?

6. What happens on weekends? Where is the center of the social scene? Do many students go off campus?

7. If the school has fraternities and sororities (or clubs), what percentage of students belong to them? What percentage don't? What is the effect of choosing to belong—or not—on an individual's social life?

8. What activities (such as lectures, concerts, dances, and informal athletics) take place on campus?

9. What facilities are available for organized athletic programs? For individual exercise? Is the college involved in intercollegiate sports? Is there a well-organized intramural program?

10. What publication, drama, choral, and music groups, etc., are available on campus?

11. What kinds of counseling and placement services are available if I need them?

12. What religious facilities and organizations are involved with the campus?

13. Are there any hidden qualities about this school that I should know? Any recent or upcoming changes?

14. What are the current social issues that students are discussing?

15. What kind of housing is available? Are all freshmen housed on campus? What percentage of students live off campus?

16. How would you describe the sense of community and school spirit at this college?

In the space below, write a few questions of your own:

COLLEGE VISIT SUMMARY SHEET

It's important to keep systematic notes on your college visits in order to refer to them later. So please, take time to sit down and write your impressions, both general and specific, of the schools you visit. After each visit, write up a summary sheet for that college so that you get your *initial* reactions on paper. If you have any questions about a particular school, share them with your counselor or parents or with the college's admissions staff. Be sure to make enough copies of this summary sheet (which ends on page 59) to cover all the colleges you visit. (Bring them with you when you go.)

College Visit Summary

Name of College:

Date of Visit:

Interviewer:

Reactions to Academic Offerings

What freshman or special programs are offered?

How serious do the students seem about academics?

What honors and/or Advanced Placement credits are available?

How successful are the students in gaining admission to professional schools?

How varied is the curriculum?

How strict or flexible are curriculum requirements?

How available are faculty members for consultation or help?

Reactions to Student Body

List your impressions of the student body in terms of appearance, style, degree of interest and enthusiasm, and diversity of social, religious, and ethnic background.

Reactions to Campus Facilities and Social Life

How complete and modern are the facilities, such as dorms (number of people to a room, furnishings, plumbing, etc.), the dining room (how is the meal plan), student center, and cultural and athletic facilities?

How active is the social life?

Do fraternities, sororities, or some other group dominate the social scene?

Are there restrictions on freshman participation in athletics?

What rules and regulations govern social life?

Is it a "suitcase," or commuter, campus?

Reactions to College Costs and Financial Aid

What is the cost of the college?

What is the availability of financial aid and the deadline date for filing the Financial Aid Form or Family Financial Statement?

Are there merit or special interest scholarships not based on need?

What are the typical costs for social activities?

Are there part-time job opportunities?

What are the projected increases in tuition and room and board for the next few years?

Overall Impressions

What were your gut likes and dislikes?

What seemed different or special?

What kind of student do you feel would be happiest there? Are you that kind of person?

Ratings

On a scale of 1 to 5 (with 1 being the highest), rate the college on the following factors:

- Academic offerings   1 2 3 4 5
- Student body   1 2 3 4 5
- Campus facilities and social life   1 2 3 4 5
- Availability of financial aid (if important to you)   1 2 3 4 5
- Overall rating   1 2 3 4 5

Other Comments

After You Return Home

If you have had a personal interview, be sure to write a thank-you note to your interviewer as soon as you return home. It does not have to be long, but you should thank the interviewer for his or her time and mention a specific thought, idea, remark, or fact that came up during your exchange of information.

Sample Thank-You Note to Your Interviewer

Your Street Address
Town, State, Zip Code
Date

Interviewer's Name
College Name
Address
Town, State, Zip Code

Dear (Mr., Mrs., or Ms.) _____:

Thank you very much for spending time with me on (date). I enjoyed meeting you and appreciated the chance to see (name of college). I especially enjoyed the opportunity to (here you can mention a specific part of the interview).

Once again, thank you for your time. It will help me in the rest of my application process to (name of college).

Sincerely,

(signature)
Your Name

By now you've met all the requirements and made all the deadlines to keep you in the running as an applicant—all but one. You still have to send completed applications to the admissions offices of your college choices. Before you can do that, however, you need to whittle down your list of colleges and universities to a manageable number and determine your order of preference. Once you've done that, filling out application and financial aid forms is all that's standing between you and notification by the schools.

This section shows you how to narrow your selection, tie up all the loose ends associated with the application, and fill out the forms. It also provides basic information on financial aid.

NARROWING THE CHOICE

Now it's "crunch" time—time to decide where you'll apply, fill out forms, write your essays, and send in money (each college charges a fee to process applications).

The first step is to narrow the field. Take stock of all the information you have accumulated to date on the twenty or so colleges you considered. Review the notes you made after your campus visits and interviews. Take a thoughtful, realistic look at yourself through the eyes of a college admissions committee. Reread the catalogs of schools you might like but didn't visit. Eliminate those colleges you know are not suitable, and create a list of four to seven schools to which you'll apply.

As you pull your list together, remember that a college must meet your academic and intellectual needs, just as you must meet its academic standards. Do not choose a college by the name game—applying because neighbors, friends, or family have heard it's a good school. No single college is the only right school for anyone, and no college is right unless it's a good place for you.

Consider early decision only if you have a definite first choice and your grades and SAT scores generally meet the standards of that college by the end of your junior year.

Be sure your final list includes at least one school where your application has a better than reasonable chance of acceptance and that this "safety" is one you would be happy to attend. There is no sense in applying to Bluebeard State if you wouldn't be caught dead there.

The List

1. _____

2. _____

3. _____

4. _____

5. _____

6. _____

7. _____

THE APPLICATION

The colleges that you're applying to have your official transcript (sent from your high school) and your standardized test scores (sent from the test centers), as well as recommendations from your teachers, guidance counselor, and/or employers. All of these offer another person's view of you. The application is *you;* it is a reflection of who you are and what you have accomplished. It is your opportunity to present yourself as you would like others to see you.

When you have selected the colleges and universities you will apply to, pull their applications from their folders and make copies of them (if you haven't already). If you're missing any forms, write or call for them now. Keep original application forms in their files and use the copies as your worksheets. Work on them until you are satisfied, then transfer the information to the original.

Many of the questions on the applications are routine and require factual information about your background. You have already gathered most of this information on your Personal Data Sheet.

Other questions deal with your goals. They may ask you to specify the academic degree that you wish to pursue. If you are unsure, don't hesitate to say "undecided." If you are interested in a specific degree and the institution asks you to write a special statement indicating why, consider that request seriously. Your comments will be read carefully in order to assess your motivation in pursuing a career in that field.

Still other questions ask you to discuss your extracurricular activities. The more selective the college, the more likely it is to use nonacademic criteria to distinguish between candidates. Colleges want to build a class composed of people with diverse talents and interests. Be honest when indicating what you have done, what leadership roles you have assumed (if any), and what activities you have been involved in. It is better to demonstrate actual involvement in a few activities than a minimal involvement in many.

Tips for Filling Out Your Application

- Be relevant and complete.

- Type or write neatly.

- Be grammatical (use correct punctuation and check your spelling) and have someone proofread your worksheet.

- Make the deadlines.

- Know yourself and be yourself.

THE ESSAY

There are two types of essay: the personal statement and one that must answer more specific questions. Some colleges ask for one or the other; some ask for both. Some allow you to choose. But no matter which essay you write, the principles of composition remain the same:

- Use specific examples from your own life and avoid generalizations.

- Depth is more important than breadth.

- Be honest.

- Be yourself.

The most difficult questions to respond to are the ones that ask, in a general way, to tell about yourself. Colleges are less interested in name, rank, and serial number than in the kind of human being you are—what kinds of experiences you've had and, even more important, what those experiences have meant to you.

For example, you may want to choose a quote that has special significance to you and reflect upon it. You may want to choose a single experience and discuss several aspects of yourself in light of it. You may want to discuss a personal philosophy that has emerged as a result of your experiences.

Your personal statement should be written, rewritten, and written again, until it truly reflects you as a person. This is the opportunity that the college gives you to describe the kinds of things you are enthusiastic about, your talents and unique experiences, your ways of demonstrating leadership, and the personal qualities you feel are important to bring to the attention of college admissions officials. Try to discuss what sets you apart from other applicants.

If colleges ask a specific question, answer what they ask. Don't stray from the topic.

Writing Tips

- Draft your essay the summer before your senior year. You *will* need the time.

- Jot down your goals and how you feel college will help you meet them *before* you begin. Look back at your list of school, community, and travel experiences. Look at your responses under "Getting to Know Yourself." Develop a one-sentence theme to describe yourself or choose a single experience that could become a vehicle for describing yourself.

- Choose the style you would like to use for your essay. Straight prose is most common and is fine, but if you want to try poetry or some other writing style, do it!

- Write a draft. Put it away for 24 hours. Read it. Is it focused? Boring? Interesting? Would you respond favorably to the person it describes?

- Rewrite it.

- Repeat the two previous steps until you like what you have written and are satisfied that it tells your story well.

- Have someone you respect read it and comment candidly on it.

- Check carefully for grammar and spelling errors.

- Read the essay aloud to hear how it reads.

- Type your essay *carefully.*

- Proofread it again and retype if necessary.

RECOMMENDATIONS

Colleges request recommendations as a way of getting additional insight into who you are, how you have gotten to this point, and where you may be headed in the future.

They don't want to be flooded with dozens of letters on your behalf—recommendations from one or two teachers will generally do, unless the college specifies something different. If you can solicit letters from teachers of different subjects or who know you in different ways (an English teacher and a coach, for instance), all the better.

Choose people who know you best, and be sure to ask them well in advance how they feel about recommending you. Character references are helpful only if the writer knows you well and can talk about a special skill, achievement, or attribute. It doesn't make sense to have the mayor write a letter for you just because he sat next to your great-aunt in the fourth grade. (However, if you worked closely with him on his last campaign, let him write one.) Waive your rights to see the letters after they are written. The results will be more honest and thus more useful.

Make sure to give the people writing recommendations plenty of time before the letters are due. You can help them by giving them a copy of the personal data sheet that

> **Choose your references wisely; ask people who know you well.**

includes your name, age, activities, and accomplishments—some of which they may be unaware of—that you've already filled out. Provide them with stamped, addressed envelopes (marked "For the File of [your name]"), and a note to remind them of their deadline. Remember to thank them!

FINANCIAL AID

Any candidate for admission to any college can, and should, apply for financial aid if his or her family feels it may not be able to pay the entire sum. In view of rising college costs at both public and private institutions, financial aid is an option for most families today.

The Financial Aid Form (FAF) and Family Financial Statement (FFS) are available from your guidance counselor. The colleges that require SAT scores generally use the FAF, which is administered by the College Scholarship Service. The FFS is the American College Testing Program counterpart and is generally used by the colleges that require ACT scores. Many colleges require their own forms be filled out, as well. If you are going to submit *any* financial aid forms, *keep well ahead of stated deadlines.*

You can get information about student aid from the Federal Student Aid Information Center by calling its toll-free number, 800-333-INFO. College financial aid officers are also excellent sources for suggestions and advice. Most institutions award a package of financial aid—a combination of grants (money that does not have to be paid back), loans (money to be paid back after college), and jobs on campus (which gives you the chance to earn money to help pay for school)—to meet financial need.

There are two basic types of financial aid. One is need-based and involves the greatest number of students who receive aid. The amount granted is determined by the difference between the cost of college and the family's ability to pay. The second type is a merit-based scholarship and is generally offered to students in recognition of academic ability, special skills, or talents—not on the basis of need.

The federal government is the largest source of student financial aid. Its funds include Pell Grants; three campus-based programs (administered by college financial aid administrators)—Perkins Loans, College Work-Study awards, and Supplemental Educational Opportunity Grants; and Stafford Loans, PLUS loans (for parents of dependent undergraduate students), and Supplemental Loans for Students, each administered by a bank, credit union, or savings and loan association. State aid is also available and includes grants, loans, and work-study programs. In addition, colleges individually provide (and control) their own sources of aid.

If you are going to apply for financial aid, follow these important steps:

- Determine your eligibility for federal programs.

- Get FAF/FFS applications from your guidance office and any other forms you need from the colleges you're applying to.

- Talk to the financial aid office at each campus to find out if you are eligible for any special programs.

- Observe *all* deadlines!

MAILING THE APPLICATION

Receipt of a completed application form is usually the first step in the creation of a folder in your name at each college to which you apply. (The other components include your high school transcript and test scores, which, if you've followed the instructions in this workbook, are on their way to those schools.) Below is a list of the things you should do to eliminate any last-minute problems before you mail your applications.

- Reread all application instructions carefully to double-check that you've followed them correctly.

- Make a photocopy of each final application for your own records.

- Send your application by registered mail (Return Receipt Requested) or include a self-addressed postcard for the admissions secretary to mail back to you when the application has been received.

- Give transcript and midyear grade report request forms to your school guidance counselor, so that the information can be mailed at the appropriate time.

- Fill out the forms available in your guidance office to forward ACT, SAT, and Achievement scores to each college you apply to if you haven't arranged for the information to be sent directly from the testing organizations.

Finally . . .

It's Your Choice

By April of your senior year, at least one of the colleges you selected will have accepted you. Now *you* must make a choice.

Go back and check your original list of priorities. You may find you've been accepted by the one school that clearly addresses all of them, which makes your decision an easy one. If that's not the case, visit the colleges that have accepted you if it's practical to do so. You'll make your visit with a different frame of reference than before; this time you *know* they want you. Be certain to look around and ask questions with an eye toward spending a few years there. Talk to college students, teachers, your guidance counselor, and friends about your alternatives. Don't get too confused or worry that you'll make the wrong choice. There's no such thing as a single "right" college. Trust yourself!

If you're on a wait list for your first-choice school, make sure you meet all the deposit deadlines for admissions and housing at your next college of choice. Let the school that has wait-listed you know (by letter) that it remains your first choice, if it does.

Finally, remember to inform the schools whose offers you turn down of your decision.

MORE OUTSTANDING TITLES FROM PETERSON'S

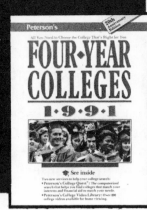

PETERSON'S GUIDE TO FOUR-YEAR COLLEGES 1991

For twenty years, students, parents, counselors, and librarians have relied on *Peterson's Guide to Four-Year Colleges* because it's the *only* college guide that provides **all** the information they need to choose the college that's best for them.

Profiling 1,950 accredited institutions that grant baccalaureate degrees in the United States and Canada, the guide includes the highest-quality and most accurate data on everything from admission requirements to campus life.

In-Depth Descriptions of the Colleges—not found in any other college guide—go beyond the data profiles to provide a full, personal look at each college. Nearly 800 of these full descriptions, written by the colleges themselves, are included—more than ever before!

Also included are college directories—on over 450 majors as well as cost, entrance difficulty, and geographic area. Together in a special section, these directories help readers find out instantly which colleges have the characteristics they're looking for.

Peterson's Guide to Four-Year Colleges also offers:

Peterson's College Quest®, a college search and financial aid questionnaire that students can send in for complete analysis by Peterson's.
Peterson's Video Library, an 800-number service to order official college videos.

Coming in July 1990, 21st Edition
$17.95 paperback
$33.95 hardcover

College Quest® is a registered trademark of Peterson's

PETERSON'S COMPETITIVE COLLEGES 1990–91

One in three of all college-bound high school students will enroll in one of the colleges listed in *Peterson's Competitive Colleges*—the most widely used and respected book on the subject.

This is the only book that identifies competitive institutions objectively—by the quality of students they attract. For academically talented students, it's the most useful college guide they can buy.

Peterson's Competitive Colleges 1990–91 is the only annual college guide published in the spring; that means juniors can take it with them when they visit campuses during the summer before their senior year.

The 1990–91 edition includes important cost and financial aid information to help students and parents understand that a more competitive college is not necessarily a more expensive college.

Each of the 331 colleges listed in the guide has a separate page devoted to the information important to high achievers, including:
- Statistics on high school achievements of the freshman class
- Attrition figures
- Percentages of graduates who pursue further study

The book includes eleven helpful directories to facilitate the search process.

Peterson's Competitive Colleges helps families discover a surprising number of less familiar institutions that can deliver the very challenges they're seeking.

$10.95 paperback

NEW

SAT PANIC PLAN

Joan Davenport Carris with Michael R. Crystal and William R. McQuade

For many, this book arrives just in time! It's the perfect solution for college-bound students who:
- Put off thinking about the SAT until the last minute
- Hate tests and preparing for them
- Are worried about the math section—or feel their vocabulary could use a boost
- Need confidence

Teaching valuable test-taking skills—not tricks or gimmicks—*SAT Panic Plan* is a two-week review to help procrastinators do all they can to prepare for the SAT in the short time left. It puts the student in control of the test—not the other way around.

Using *SAT Panic Plan*, students will learn:
- How to score more right answers
- Why, when, and how to guess
- Logic and reasoning techniques for mathematics and verbal questions
- Fast, intelligent approaches to the four types of verbal questions

SAT Panic Plan features a full-length practice SAT so students can familiarize themselves with the format. A 400-word vocabulary list is included.

Coming in September 1990
$7.95 paperback

Look for these and other Peterson's titles in your local bookstore

Test Scorecard

Use the charts below to keep track of the tests you take. Mark the date each test was taken and the score you earned in the appropriate boxes. Use the Application Checklist that appears on the inside back cover to indicate that test results have been sent to the appropriate colleges or universities.

	PSAT	PSAT
Date Taken		
Verbal		
Math		

	SAT	SAT	SAT
Date Taken			
Verbal			
Math			

	ACT	ACT
Date Taken		
English		
Math		
Reading		
Science Reasoning		
Composite Score		

	ACH	ACH
Date Taken		
American History and Social Studies		
Biology		
Chemistry		
English Composition with essay ☐ without essay ☐ (check one)		
European History and World Cultures		
Languages French ☐ German ☐ Italian ☐ Latin ☐ Modern Hebrew ☐ Spanish ☐ (check whichever apply)		
Literature I ☐ II ☐ (check one)		
Math		
Physics		